Fredrick Wonders

How To Get Millions Of Followers On Facebook

Mastering the Art of Building a Massive and Engaging Facebook Audience

This book was professionally typeset on Reedsy
Find out more at reedsy.com

Dedication

*To my family and friends, whose unwavering support and
encouragement have been my greatest inspiration. Your
belief in me has made this journey possible.*

Fredrick Wonders

Epigraph

"Success on social media is not about reaching millions; it's about connecting deeply with the ones who matter."

Fredrick   Wonders

Contents

1.

2.

3.

4.

5.

6.

7.

8.

9.

10.

11.

12.

Foreword

Foreword

The rise of social media has fundamentally transformed the way we communicate, share information, and build communities. Among the various platforms available today, Facebook remains a dominant force, offering unparalleled opportunities for personal and professional growth. Yet, amidst the sheer volume of content and competition, achieving a significant following on Facebook can seem daunting.

When I first started my journey in the world of social media, I was overwhelmed by the complexities of Facebook's algorithms, the challenge of creating engaging content, and the constant need to adapt to new features and trends. Through trial and error, extensive research, and learning from industry experts, I discovered the strategies that truly work. These insights enabled me to grow my own audience and help others do the same.

I had the privilege of seeing firsthand how the techniques shared in this book transformed pages from obscurity to prominence. The strategies compiled here are not just theoretical concepts; they are actionable steps backed by data, real-world experience, and success stories.

This book, "How to Get Millions of Followers on Facebook: A Comprehensive Guide," is a testament to the power of perseverance, creativity, and strategic thinking. It's a valuable resource for anyone looking to build a substantial and engaged following on Facebook, regardless of their starting point. Whether you're a business owner aiming to reach new customers, an influencer seeking to amplify your voice, or simply someone passionate about connecting with others, this guide provides the blueprint for achieving your goals.

In a world where digital presence can significantly impact success, understanding how to leverage Facebook effectively is crucial. The journey outlined in these pages will take you through the essential aspects of Facebook growth—from mastering algorithms to crafting compelling content, engaging with your audience, and utilizing paid advertising for maximum reach. You'll learn how to analyze your performance, refine your strategy, and maintain your growth in an ever-changing digital landscape.

I am excited to introduce you to this comprehensive guide and confident that the knowledge within these pages will empower you to unlock your potential on Facebook. The path to millions of followers is not just about numbers; it's about building a vibrant, engaged community that supports and grows with you.

Dive in, apply these strategies, and watch your Facebook presence flourish. The future of your social media success starts here.

With admiration and best wishes,

Fredrick   Wonders

Preface

Preface

In today's digital age, social media has become an essential tool for personal branding, business growth, and community building. Among the myriad of platforms available, Facebook stands out as a titan, boasting billions of active users worldwide. The potential for reaching and influencing a vast audience on Facebook is unparalleled, but achieving significant success on this platform requires more than just sporadic posts and occasional interactions.

This book, "How to Get Millions of Followers on Facebook: A Comprehensive Guide," is born out of the need to demystify the process of growing a substantial and engaged following on Facebook. Whether you're an entrepreneur looking to expand your business, an influencer aiming to amplify your voice, or a social media enthusiast eager to make an impact, this guide is designed to provide you with the tools and knowledge necessary to achieve your goals.

As someone who has spent years studying the intricacies of social media dynamics, I understand the challenges and frustrations that come with trying to stand out in a crowded digital landscape. The strategies and insights shared in this book are not theoretical concepts, but practical, tested, and proven methods that have helped countless individuals and businesses attain remarkable success on Facebook.

In the following chapters, you will embark on a journey that covers every aspect of Facebook growth—from understanding the platform's algorithms to creating engaging content, leveraging paid advertising, and building a loyal community. You will learn how to analyze your performance, adapt to changes, and sustain your growth over time. Each chapter is designed to equip you with actionable steps, real-world examples, and valuable tips to guide you toward your objective of gaining millions of followers.

The digital world is ever-evolving, and staying ahead requires continuous learning and adaptation. My hope is that this book will serve as a comprehensive resource, empowering you to navigate the complexities of Facebook with confidence and creativity.

Thank you for choosing this guide as your companion on your journey to social media success. I am excited to share this knowledge with you and look forward to seeing the incredible heights you will reach.

To your success,

Fredrick   Wonders

Acknowledgement

Acknowledgement

Creating "How to Get Millions of Followers on Facebook: A Comprehensive Guide" has been an enlightening journey, and it would not have been possible without the support, guidance, and encouragement of many individuals.

First and foremost, I would like to express my deepest gratitude to my family and friends for their unwavering support and understanding throughout the writing process. Your patience and encouragement have been invaluable.

A special thanks to the social media experts, influencers, and marketers who generously shared their insights and experiences with me. Your wisdom and expertise have greatly enriched this book and provided real-world perspectives that are essential for success on Facebook.

I am immensely grateful to my editor, whose keen eye for detail and dedication to excellence have significantly enhanced the quality of this book. Your constructive feedback and meticulous editing have been crucial in shaping the final manuscript.

Thank you to my publisher for believing in this project and providing the resources and platform to bring this guide to life. Your support has been instrumental in making this book a reality.

I would also like to acknowledge the vibrant community of social media enthusiasts and professionals who continue to inspire me. Your passion for innovation and knowledge-sharing drives the industry forward and motivates me to keep learning and growing.

Finally, to the readers of this book—thank you for embarking on this journey with me. Your desire to learn and succeed on Facebook is the driving force behind this work. I hope the strategies and insights shared here empower you to achieve remarkable growth and engagement on your Facebook page.

To everyone who has contributed to this book in any way, your support and encouragement mean the world to me. This book is a testament to the power of collaboration, and I am deeply grateful for your contributions.

With heartfelt thanks,

Fredrick   Wonders

1

Understanding the Facebook Ecosystem

Understanding the Facebook Ecosystem

1.1 The Power of Facebook

Facebook is one of the largest social media platforms in the world, with billions of active users. This massive audience provides an unparalleled opportunity for individuals and businesses to reach and engage with potential followers. Understanding Facebook's potential can help you leverage its power to build a significant following.

1.2 Setting Realistic Goals

Before diving into strategies for growth, it's essential to set realistic and measurable goals. These could include increasing follower count by a certain percentage, achieving a specific engagement rate, or driving traffic to a website. Clear goals provide direction and a benchmark for success.

1.3 Understanding the Facebook Algorithm

The Facebook algorithm determines which posts appear in users' feeds, prioritizing content based on relevance and engagement. Key factors influencing the algorithm include:

Engagement: Likes, comments, shares, and other interactions.

Relevance: How relevant the content is to the user based on past behavior.

Timeliness: Newer posts are often given priority.

Content Type: Different content types (videos, images, links) may be prioritized differently.

Understanding these factors can help you tailor your content to maximize visibility.

1.4 Identifying Your Target Audience

To effectively grow your following, you need to know who you're trying to reach. This involves defining your target audience based on demographics (age, gender, location) and psychographics (interests, behaviors). Creating detailed audience personas can help you tailor your content and engagement strategies.

1.5 Competitor Analysis

Studying successful pages in your niche can provide valuable insights. Analyze competitors' content, engagement strategies, and posting frequency. Identify what works well for them and think about how you can apply similar tactics, while also identifying gaps or opportunities they might be missing.

The groundwork for building a large following on Facebook by highlighting the platform's power, the importance of setting clear goals, understanding the algorithm, identifying your target audience, and learning from competitors,by mastering these foundational elements, you'll be better prepared to implement effective growth strategies in subsequent   chapters.

2

Building a Strong Foundation

Building a Strong Foundation

2.1 Creating an Attractive Profile

Your Facebook profile is the first impression visitors get, so it needs to be visually appealing and professional.

Profile Picture: Choose a high-quality image that represents your brand. For businesses, this could be your logo. For personal brands, use a professional headshot.

Cover Photo: Utilize this space to highlight your brand's personality. It could showcase a product, a slogan, or an event.

2.2 Optimizing Your Page Information

Your page's information section is crucial for searchability and providing essential details about your brand.

Bio: Write a concise and compelling bio that clearly states who you are and what you do. Use keywords relevant to your niche.

Contact Information: Ensure your contact details are up to date so followers can easily reach you.

Additional Information: Fill out all sections, including location, website, and hours of operation if applicable.

2.3 Setting Up Page Tabs and Templates

Customize your page tabs and layout to enhance user experience and provide easy access to important sections.

Tabs: Organize your tabs (e.g., Home, About, Photos, Videos, Events) to suit your content and audience.

Templates: Use Facebook's page templates designed for different types of businesses (e.g., Shopping, Services, Venues) to optimize your page layout.

2.4 Establishing a Content Calendar

Consistency is key to maintaining and growing your follower base.

Planning: Create a content calendar to plan your posts ahead of time. Include a mix of content types (videos, images, text) to keep your feed interesting.

Frequency: Determine a posting frequency that keeps your audience engaged without overwhelming them. Consistency helps in staying top-of-mind.

2.5 Ensuring Accessibility

Making your page accessible ensures you reach a wider audience, including those with disabilities.

Alt Text: Use alt text for images so that screen readers can describe the images to visually impaired users.

Captions: Provide captions for videos to assist hearing-impaired users.

Clear Design: Ensure your page design is easy to navigate and read.

By creating an attractive profile, optimizing page information, customizing tabs and templates, establishing a content calendar, and ensuring accessibility, you lay the groundwork for effective engagement and growth.

3

Creating Engaging Content

Creating Engaging Content

3.1 Content Types and Their Importance

Different types of content can engage your audience in various ways. Understanding their strengths and weaknesses helps in crafting a balanced content strategy.

Text Posts: Great for sharing quick updates, thoughts, and engaging in conversations.

Images: Visually appealing and can quickly capture attention. Ideal for showcasing products, behind-the-scenes glimpses, and infographics.

Videos: Highly engaging and shareable. Use videos for tutorials, product demos, and storytelling.

Live Streams: Real-time engagement. Use live streams for Q&A sessions, behind-the-scenes looks, and events.

Stories: Short-lived but highly engaging. Perfect for quick updates, promotions, and polls.

3.2 Crafting High-Quality Posts

Creating content that resonates with your audience requires attention to detail and creativity.

Headlines and Captions: Write compelling headlines and captions that grab attention and encourage engagement. Use questions, intriguing statements, or calls to action.

Visual Quality: Use high-quality images and videos. Poor visuals can deter engagement.

Consistency in Branding: Ensure your content aligns with your brand's voice, style, and messaging.

3.3 Leveraging User-Generated Content

User-generated content (UGC) can boost engagement and foster a sense of community.

Encouraging UGC: Ask your followers to share their experiences, photos, and stories related to your brand.

Showcasing UGC: Feature user-generated content on your page, giving credit to the original creators. This not only provides fresh content but also encourages others to contribute.

3.4 Storytelling Techniques

Storytelling can create an emotional connection with your audience, making your content more memorable and shareable.

Personal Stories: Share personal anecdotes or stories from your brand's journey.

Customer Stories: Highlight stories from satisfied customers or clients.

Narrative Structure: Use a clear beginning, middle, and end to craft engaging stories.

3.5 Utilizing Facebook Live

Facebook Live is a powerful tool for real-time interaction with your audience.

Planning: Plan your live sessions in advance. Promote them ahead of time to build anticipation.

Engagement: Interact with viewers by answering questions and responding to comments in real-time.

Recaps: After the live session, share a recap or highlights to keep the conversation going.

By understanding the importance of different content types, crafting high-quality posts, leveraging user-generated content, employing storytelling techniques, and utilizing Facebook Live, you can create a dynamic and engaging presence on Facebook. This content strategy forms the heart of your efforts to grow a large, loyal following.

4

Growing Your Audience Organically

Growing Your Audience Organically

4.1 Engaging with Your Community

Building a strong community is essential for organic growth.

Active Interaction: Respond promptly to comments and messages. Show appreciation for your followers by liking and replying to their posts.

Fostering Discussions: Encourage discussions by asking open-ended questions and creating posts that invite opinions and stories.

Creating a Sense of Belonging: Make your followers feel valued by acknowledging their contributions and featuring them on your page.

4.2 Collaborating with Influencers

Influencer collaborations can introduce your page to a broader audience.

Identifying Relevant Influencers: Find influencers whose audience aligns with your target demographic.

Building Relationships: Engage with influencers by commenting on their posts and sharing their content. Approach them with collaboration ideas that provide mutual benefits.

Leveraging Influencer Content:Co-create content with influencers, such as interviews, takeovers, or joint live sessions, to tap into their follower base.

4.3 Running Contests and Giveaways

Contests and giveaways can significantly boost your follower count and engagement.

Designing Engaging Contests:Create contests that are fun and relevant to your audience. Ensure the rules are clear and the prizes are attractive.

Encouraging Participation: Make participation easy and engaging. For example, require participants to like your page, share your post, or tag friends.

Promoting Your Contests: Use Facebook Ads, influencer partnerships, and cross-promotion on other platforms to maximize reach.

4.4 Cross-Promoting on Other Platforms

Leveraging your presence on other social media platforms can drive traffic to your Facebook page.

Consistent Branding: Maintain a consistent brand voice and style across all platforms.

Encouraging Followers to Connect:Regularly invite your followers on other platforms to join your Facebook page by highlighting exclusive content or special offers.

Utilizing Platform Strengths: Use the strengths of each platform to promote your Facebook page. For instance, use

Instagram Stories or Twitter threads to share compelling reasons to follow you on Facebook.

4.5 Utilizing Hashtags and Trends

Strategic use of hashtags and trending topics can increase your content's visibility.

Researching Hashtags: Identify popular and relevant hashtags in your niche. Use tools like Hashtagify or Facebook's own search feature to discover trending hashtags.

Creating Branded Hashtags: Develop unique hashtags for your brand and encourage your followers to use them.

Participating in Trends: Stay updated with current trends and participate in relevant conversations. Create timely content that aligns with trending topics to increase your reach.

By engaging with your community, collaborating with influencers, running contests and giveaways, cross-promoting on other platforms, and utilizing hashtags and trends, you can expand your follower base naturally. These methods help build a loyal and engaged audience, laying the foundation for sustained growth and success on the platform.

5

Leveraging Paid Advertising

Leveraging Paid Advertising

5.1 Understanding Facebook Ads

Facebook Ads can accelerate your growth by reaching a larger, targeted audience.

Ad Types: Familiarize yourself with various ad types, including photo ads, video ads, carousel ads, slideshow ads, and collection ads. Each type has its strengths and best use cases.

Ad Objectives: Determine your ad campaign's objective, such as increasing page likes, driving website traffic, or boosting post engagement.

5.2 Setting Up Your First Ad Campaign

Creating a successful ad campaign involves careful planning and execution.

Campaign Objective: Choose an objective that aligns with your goals. Common objectives include brand awareness, engagement, and conversions.

Target Audience: Define your target audience based on demographics, interests, behaviors, and location. Use Facebook's Audience Insights tool to refine your targeting.

Budget and Schedule: Set a budget that suits your goals and determine the duration of your campaign. You can choose between daily and lifetime budgets.

5.3 Crafting Effective Ad Copy and Creative

High-quality ad copy and visuals are crucial for capturing attention and driving action.

Compelling Copy: Write clear, concise, and engaging ad copy. Use strong calls to action that encourage users to engage with your ad.

Eye-Catching Visuals: Use high-quality images or videos that align with your brand and message. Ensure your visuals are attention-grabbing and relevant to your target audience.

Ad Format: Choose the ad format that best showcases your content. For example, carousel ads are great for highlighting multiple products, while video ads are ideal for storytelling.

5.4 A/B Testing and Optimization

A/B testing helps you identify the most effective elements of your ads and optimize for better performance.

Creating Variations: Develop multiple versions of your ad with slight variations in copy, visuals, or targeting.

Testing: Run these variations simultaneously to see which performs best. Use Facebook's Split Testing feature to manage this process.

Analyzing Results: Monitor the performance of each variation. Identify which elements drive the best results and use this data to optimize future ads.

5.5 Analyzing Ad Performance

Regularly analyzing your ad performance is key to refining your strategy and maximizing ROI.

Facebook Insights: Use Facebook Insights to track key metrics such as reach, engagement, click-through rate (CTR), and conversion rate.

Data-Driven Decisions: Use the data from your ad performance to make informed decisions. Adjust your targeting, ad copy, visuals, and budget based on what's working.

Continuous Improvement: Continuously test and optimize your ads to improve performance over time. Stay updated with Facebook's latest ad features and best practices.

By understanding the different types of ads, setting up effective campaigns, crafting compelling ad copy and visuals, conducting A/B testing, and analyzing ad performance, you can create powerful ad strategies that drive significant growth and engagement. Paid advertising, when done correctly, can be a game-changer in rapidly expanding your follower base and achieving your goals on Facebook.

6

Utilizing Facebook Groups

Utilizing Facebook Groups

6.1 Creating and Growing a Facebook Group

Facebook Groups offer a unique way to build a community around your brand and engage with your audience on a deeper level.

Creating a Group: Start by defining the purpose and niche of your group. Choose a relevant and searchable name, and set clear group rules and guidelines.

Growing Your Group: Invite your existing followers and encourage them to invite their friends. Promote your group on your Facebook page, other social media platforms, and email newsletters.

6.2 Engaging Group Members

Keeping your group active and engaged is crucial for its success.

Regular Posts: Share valuable content regularly, including tips, articles, questions, and exclusive updates. Use a content calendar to stay consistent.

Encouraging Participation: Ask open-ended questions, create polls, and host discussions to encourage members to share their thoughts and experiences.

Member Spotlights: Highlight active members and their contributions to foster a sense of community and appreciation.

6.3 Leveraging Groups for Page Growth

Your Facebook Group can be a powerful tool for driving traffic to your main page.

Cross-Promotion: Regularly share updates and posts from your main page within the group. Encourage group members to like and follow your page for more content.

Exclusive Content: Offer group members exclusive content, such as behind-the-scenes looks or early access to new products, to incentivize them to follow your main page.

6.4 Moderation and Community Guidelines

Effective moderation ensures a positive and productive environment in your group.

Setting Rules: Clearly define and communicate group rules regarding behavior, promotion, and content sharing. Pin these rules to the top of the group.

Active Moderation: Monitor posts and comments regularly. Address any issues promptly, and be consistent in enforcing rules.

Building a Moderation Team: As your group grows, consider appointing trusted members as moderators to help manage the community.

6.5 Hosting Group Events and Activities

Organizing events and activities can keep your group vibrant and engaging.

Virtual Events: Host live Q&A sessions, webinars, or workshops within the group. Promote these events in advance to maximize attendance.

Challenges and Activities: Create fun challenges or activities that encourage members to participate and engage with each other. Examples include photo contests, themed discussions, or collaborative projects.

Recap and Feedback: After each event or activity, share a recap and ask for feedback to improve future events.

By creating and growing a group, engaging members, leveraging the group for page growth, enforcing moderation and community guidelines, and hosting events and activities, you can foster a vibrant community that supports and enhances your brand's presence on Facebook. This deeper level of engagement can drive long-term loyalty and organic growth, further solidifying your success on the platform.

7

Analytics and Insights

Analytics and Insights

7.1 Understanding Facebook Insights

F acebook Insights provides a wealth of data to help you understand your page's performance and audience behavior.

Overview Tab: This tab gives a snapshot of your page's key metrics, such as page views, likes, reach, and post engagement. Regularly reviewing this data helps you stay informed about overall performance.

Posts Tab: Here, you can see the performance of individual posts, including reach, engagement, and interactions. Use this data to identify which types of content resonate most with your audience.

Audience Insights: This section provides demographic data about your followers, such as age, gender, location, and interests. Understanding your audience helps tailor your content to their preferences.

7.2 Analyzing Audience Data

Deeply understanding your audience is crucial for effective content and engagement strategies.

Demographics: Look at the age, gender, and location breakdown of your audience to ensure your content is relevant to your primary demographic.

Interests and Behavior: Analyze the interests and online behavior of your followers to create content that aligns with their preferences.

Engagement Patterns: Identify the times and days when your audience is most active to optimize your posting schedule for maximum reach and engagement.

7.3 Measuring Content Performance

Evaluating the performance of your content helps you refine your strategy for better results.

Engagement Metrics: Track likes, comments, shares, and reactions to understand which posts generate the most interaction.

Reach and Impressions: Measure how many people see your content and how often it appears in their feeds.

Click-Through Rate (CTR): For posts with links, monitor the CTR to see how effective your calls to action are in driving traffic to your website or other platforms.

7.4 Adjusting Your Strategy Based on Data

Use the insights gathered to make data-driven decisions and adjust your strategy.

Content Optimization: Focus on creating more of the content that performs well, and experiment with new types based on audience preferences.

Timing Adjustments: Schedule your posts for times when your audience is most active to increase visibility and engagement.

Targeting Refinements: Use audience insights to refine your targeting in both organic and paid strategies, ensuring your content reaches the most relevant users.

7.5 Reporting and Benchmarking

Regular reporting and benchmarking help track your progress and set goals for improvement.

Monthly Reports: Create detailed monthly reports summarizing key metrics and insights. Include data on reach, engagement, follower growth, and content performance.

Benchmarking: Compare your performance against industry benchmarks or competitor pages to understand your standing and identify areas for improvement.

Goal Setting: Use your reports and benchmarks to set realistic, measurable goals for future growth and engagement.

By understanding and utilizing Facebook Insights, analyzing audience data, measuring content performance, adjusting your strategy based on data, and regularly reporting and benchmarking, you can make informed decisions that enhance your page's effectiveness. This data-driven approach ensures you continually refine your tactics for optimal results and   sustained   growth.

8

Enhancing Engagement

Enhancing Engagement

8.1 Creating Interactive Content

Interactive content keeps your audience engaged and encourages active participation.

Polls and Surveys: Use Facebook's poll feature to ask questions and gather opinions from your followers. Surveys can provide deeper insights into their preferences and needs.

Quizzes: Create fun and relevant quizzes that entertain your audience while providing insights into their interests.

Interactive Videos: Use Facebook Live or video posts to engage with your audience in real-time. Encourage viewers to comment and ask questions during the broadcast.

8.2 Hosting Contests and Giveaways

Contests and giveaways can significantly boost engagement and attract new followers.

Designing Engaging Contests: Plan contests that are fun, easy to enter, and offer attractive prizes. Common types include photo contests, caption contests, and referral contests.

Promoting Your Contests: Use eye-catching graphics and compelling copy to promote your contests. Leverage Facebook Ads, cross-promotion on other platforms, and partnerships with influencers to maximize reach.

Following Up: Announce winners publicly and encourage them to share their excitement on their profiles. This can lead to additional organic reach and engagement.

8.3 Building a Sense of Community

Creating a strong sense of community around your page encourages long-term engagement and loyalty.

Personal Engagement: Address your followers by name when responding to comments and messages. Show genuine interest in their thoughts and experiences.

Highlighting Followers: Feature testimonials, stories, and user-generated content from your followers. This not only provides fresh content but also makes your followers feel valued.

Hosting Meetups and Events: Organize online and offline events where your followers can interact with you and each other. These can be webinars, live Q&A sessions, or local meetups.

8.4 Leveraging Stories and Reels

Stories and Reels are powerful tools for keeping your content fresh and engaging.

Stories: Share behind-the-scenes content, daily updates, and quick tips in a format that disappears after 24 hours. Use interactive features like polls, questions, and countdowns to engage your audience.

Reels: Create short, engaging videos that are easily digestible. Use Reels to showcase products, share quick tutorials, or highlight user-generated content.

8.5 Encouraging User-Generated Content

User-generated content (UGC) can increase engagement and build trust with your audience.

Asking for Contributions: Encourage your followers to share their experiences, photos, and stories related to your brand. Use specific hashtags to organize and find UGC.

Featuring UGC: Regularly showcase user-generated content on your page. Give credit to the original creators and express appreciation for their contributions.

Creating Challenges: Launch challenges that prompt your followers to create and share content. Examples include photo challenges, DIY projects, or themed weeks.

By creating a dynamic and interactive environment, you can keep your audience actively involved and foster a sense of community. Encouraging user-generated content further strengthens the connection between your brand and its followers, driving long-term loyalty and sustained engagement.

9

Collaborations and Partnerships

Collaborations and Partnerships

9.1 Identifying Potential Partners

Collaborations and partnerships can expand your reach and introduce your brand to new audiences.

Relevant Brands and Influencers: Look for brands and influencers whose audience aligns with your target demographic. Ensure their values and content style match yours to maintain authenticity.

Complementary Services or Products: Find partners offering complementary services or products that can provide mutual benefits. For instance, a fitness influencer might partner with a health food brand.

9.2 Approaching Potential Partners

Effectively approaching potential partners involves clear communication and a compelling pitch.

Building Relationships: Start by engaging with their content—like, comment, and share their posts. Establish a rapport before proposing a collaboration.

Crafting a Compelling Proposal: Clearly outline the benefits of the partnership for both parties. Highlight your audience size, engagement rates, and any unique value propositions.

Offering Mutual Benefits: Ensure the collaboration offers value to both parties. This could be in the form of increased exposure, shared resources, or co-created content.

9.3 Types of Collaborations

Different types of collaborations can help you reach new audiences and add variety to your content.

Guest Posts and Takeovers: Invite partners to create guest posts or take over your page for a day. This introduces their followers to your page and vice versa.

Joint Contests and Giveaways: Run joint contests or giveaways with your partners. This can increase visibility and engagement for both parties.

Co-Branded Content: Create co-branded content, such as videos, blog posts, or social media campaigns. This allows you to leverage each other's strengths and audiences.

9.4 Measuring Collaboration Success

Measuring the success of your collaborations helps you understand their impact and refine future efforts.

Key Metrics: Track metrics such as follower growth, engagement rates, and reach. Compare these metrics before and after the collaboration.

Qualitative Feedback: Gather feedback from your audience about the collaboration. This can provide insights into what worked well and what could be improved.

ROI Analysis: Evaluate the return on investment (ROI) of the collaboration. Consider both the tangible results (e.g., increased followers, sales) and intangible benefits (e.g., brand awareness, networking).

9.5 Maintaining Long-Term Partnerships

Building and maintaining long-term partnerships can lead to sustained growth and success.

Regular Communication: Keep the lines of communication open with your partners. Regularly check in to discuss ongoing projects, new ideas, and feedback.

Mutual Support: Continue to support each other's content and initiatives. Share their posts, provide shout-outs, and engage with their audience.

Exploring New Opportunities: Look for new ways to collaborate and innovate. This could involve expanding into new content formats, hosting joint events, or creating exclusive offers for each other's audiences.

By identifying potential partners, effectively approaching them, exploring various types of collaborations, measuring success, and maintaining long-term partnerships, you can leverage the strengths and audiences of others to achieve mutual growth. Strategic collaborations can introduce your brand to new followers, increase engagement, and provide fresh, engaging content for your audience.

10

Sustaining Growth and Adapting to Change

Sustaining Growth and Adapting to Change

10.1 Continuously Engaging with Your Audience

Sustained growth requires ongoing engagement and interaction with your audience.

Regular Updates: Keep your audience informed with regular posts, updates, and announcements. Consistency helps maintain interest and engagement.

Active Listening: Pay attention to feedback, comments, and messages from your followers. Address their concerns, answer their questions, and show appreciation for their support.

Community Building: Continue fostering a sense of community by organizing events, creating exclusive content, and highlighting active members.

10.2 Staying Updated with Platform Changes

Facebook frequently updates its algorithms, features, and policies. Staying informed is crucial for maintaining your page's performance.

Following Official Channels: Subscribe to Facebook's official blog and follow their updates to stay informed about changes and new features.

Industry News: Keep an eye on social media industry news and trends. Websites like Social Media Examiner and HubSpot often provide valuable insights.

Testing New Features: Experiment with new features and formats as they become available. Early adoption can give you a competitive edge.

10.3 Adapting Your Strategy

As your page grows and Facebook evolves, your strategy should also adapt.

Reviewing Analytics: Regularly review your page's analytics to identify what's working and what isn't. Use this data to refine your strategy and make informed decisions.

Adjusting Content: Based on performance data and audience feedback, adjust your content types, posting schedule, and engagement tactics.

Flexibility: Be flexible and open to change. What worked initially might not always be effective, so be willing to pivot your approach when necessary.

10.4 Scaling Your Efforts

Scaling your efforts involves expanding your reach and capabilities to support continued growth.

Team Building: As your page grows, consider building a team to manage different aspects, such as content creation, community management, and advertising.

Investing in Tools: Use social media management tools like Hootsuite, Buffer, or Sprout Social to streamline your efforts and improve efficiency.

Expanding Platforms: Consider expanding your presence to other social media platforms to diversify your audience and drive traffic back to your Facebook page.

10.5 Long-Term Vision and Goals

Having a long-term vision and setting clear goals will guide your sustained growth.

Goal Setting: Set specific, measurable, achievable, relevant, and time-bound (SMART) goals for your Facebook page. These goals could include follower milestones, engagement rates, or conversion metrics.

Vision Statement: Develop a vision statement that outlines your long-term objectives and the impact you aim to achieve with your Facebook presence.

Regular Evaluation: Periodically evaluate your progress towards these goals and adjust your strategy as needed to stay on track.

By continuously engaging with your audience, staying updated with platform changes, adapting your strategy, scaling your efforts, and having a long-term vision and goals, you can ensure ongoing success on Facebook. The digital landscape is ever-evolving, and maintaining flexibility and a proactive approach will help you navigate changes and continue growing your follower base. This final chapter reinforces the need for perseverance, adaptability, and strategic planning in achieving long-term success on Facebook.

www.ingramcontent.com/pod-product-compliance
Lightning Source LLC
Chambersburg PA
CBHW072000210526
45479CB00003B/1005